A Pet's Life

Goldfish

Anita Ganeri

Heinemann Library
Chicago, Illinois

© 2003 Heinemann Library
a division of Reed Elsevier Inc.
Chicago, Illinois

Customer Service 888-454-2279

Visit our website at www.heinemannlibrary.com

Designed by Richard Parker and Tinstar Design
    Limited (www.tinstar.co.uk)
Originated by Dot Gradations
Printed and bound in China by South China Printing Company

07 06 05 04 03
10 9 8 7 6 5 4 3 2 1

**Library of Congress
Cataloging-in-Publication Data**
Ganeri, Anita, 1961-
  Goldfish / Anita Ganeri.
      v. cm. -- (A pet's life) (Heinemann first library)
Includes bibliographical references (p.   ).
Contents: What is a goldfish? -- Goldfish babies -- Your pet goldfish -- Choosing your goldfish -- Setting up your tank -- Putting in plants -- Welcome home -- Feeding time -- Cleaning the tank -- Growing up -- A healthy goldfish -- Old age.
  ISBN 1-4034-3998-2 (hardcover) -- ISBN 1-4034-4271-1 (pbk.) 1. Goldfish--Juvenile literature. [1. Goldfish. 2. Pets.] I. Title. II. Series.
  SF458.G6G36 2003
  639.3'7484--dc21
                                          2002151595

Acknowledgments
The author and publishers are grateful to the following for permission to reproduce copyright material: p. 4 Alamy Images; pp. 5 Corbis/Robert Pickett; p. 6 DK Images; p. 7 Getty Images/Photodisc; pp. 8, 9, 10, 14, 16, 17, 18, 19, 20, 24 Haddon Davies; p. 11 Corbis/Michael Keller; pp. 12, 13, 15, 21 Tudor Photography; p. 23 Corbis/Michael Boys; p. 22 RSPCA; p. 25 Dave Bevan; p. 26 Alamy; p. 27 Dave Bradford.

Cover photograph reproduced with permission of Photomax.

The publishers would like to thank Jacque Schultz, CPDT, Lila Miller, DVM, and Stephen Zawistowski, Ph.D., CAAB of the ASPCA™ for their assistance in the preparation of this book.

Every effort has been made to contact copyright holders of any material reproduced in this book. Any omissions will be rectified in subsequent printings if notice is given to the publishers.

ASPCA™ and The American Society for the Prevention of Cruelty to Animals™ are registered trademarks of The American Society for the Prevention of Cruelty to Animals.

Some words are shown in bold, **like this.** You can find out what they mean by looking in the glossary.

Contents

What Is a Goldfish?

A goldfish is a type of fish that lives in cold water. People have kept goldfish as pets for years.

Goldfish come in different shapes and sizes.

Here you can see the different parts of a goldfish's body and what each part is used for.

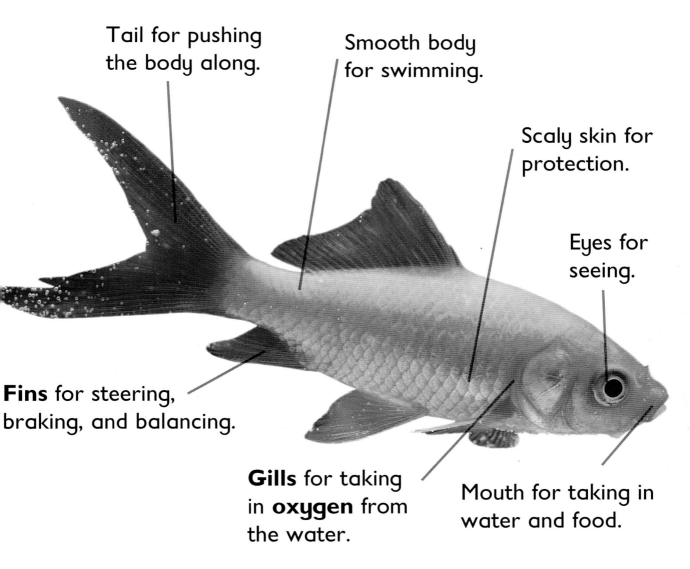

Tail for pushing the body along.

Smooth body for swimming.

Scaly skin for protection.

Eyes for seeing.

Fins for steering, braking, and balancing.

Gills for taking in **oxygen** from the water.

Mouth for taking in water and food.

Goldfish Babies

Goldfish **hatch** from eggs. A female lays thousands of eggs in water. The eggs are sticky and look like blobs of white jelly.

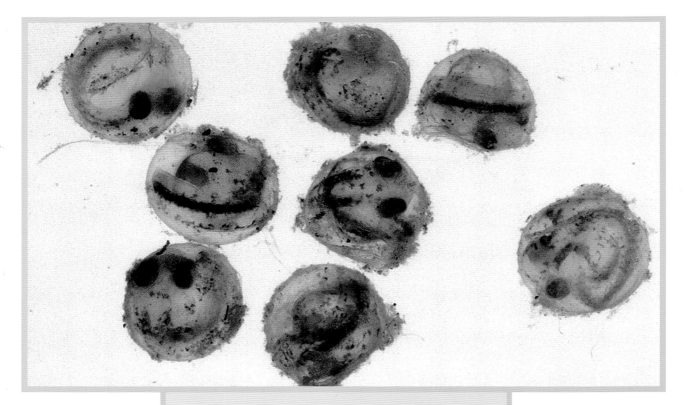

Goldfish eggs are the size of pinheads. They stick to plants.

Baby goldfish are called fry. They are colorless when they hatch. It takes the fry about four months to grow into adult goldfish. Their bodies are then a dark color.

A goldfish becomes shiny orange at about six months old.

Your Pet Goldfish

Goldfish make great pets and are fun to keep. But you must care for them properly.

Your goldfish will depend on you for all of its needs.

If you go away on vacation, make sure that someone looks after your goldfish. Ask a friend or neighbor to come over every day.

Always make sure that your goldfish has the right food and that its tank is clean.

Choosing Your Goldfish

You should buy your goldfish from a good pet store. Goldfish that you win as a prize may not be healthy.

Watch the fish swimming to check that they are healthy.

Choose a fish with bright, clear eyes and shiny skin. It should not swim slowly or have split or drooping **fins.** If you see a fish like this, it is probably not healthy.

A healthy fish should be active and have upright fins.

Setting Up the Tank

Your fish needs a tank in which to live. A tank that holds ten gallons of water will have room for two small fish.

Place your tank away from bright sunlight.

The tank should be set up 24 hours before you bring your fish home. Put **gravel** from the pet store into the bottom of the tank. Then you can fill the tank with water from the sink.

Ask an adult to help you attach a water **filter** to the tank. It will keep the water clean. A filter will also remove things in the water that might hurt your fish.

Putting in Plants

It is a good idea to put some water plants into your tank. You can dig small holes in the **gravel** and push in the plants.

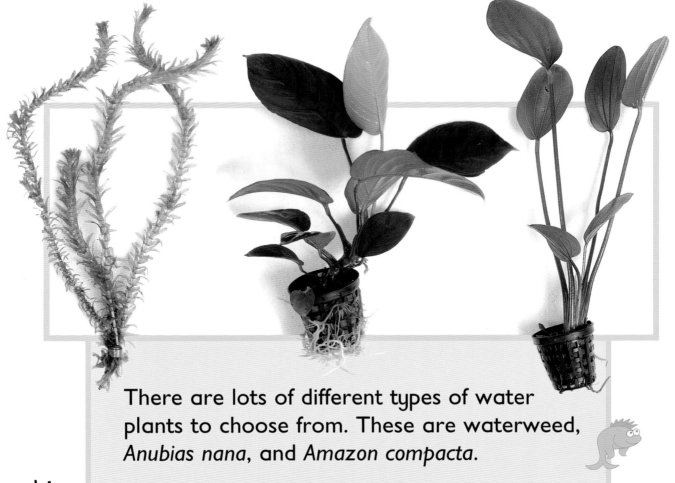

There are lots of different types of water plants to choose from. These are waterweed, *Anubias nana*, and *Amazon compacta*.

Plants are useful because they make **oxygen** for your fish to breathe. Your fish will also like to swim and find hiding places among the leaves of the plants.

Plants look best in groups, with the taller ones at the back.

Welcome Home

You can carry your goldfish home in a plastic bag of water, with space for air. You should float the bag of goldfish in the tank for 20 minutes.

When you need to move your fish, do not touch them with your hands. Use a net or jug.

This makes sure that the water **temperature** in the bag is the same as it is in the tank. Then let your goldfish out of the bag.

If you let your goldfish into the tank right away, the different water temperatures will make the goldfish sick.

Feeding Time

You can buy special goldfish food from a pet store. You can also give goldfish some chopped lettuce or spinach leaves.

Special fish flakes give your fish all the **nutrients** they need.

Feed your fish every morning and evening.
Be careful not to give your fish too much food.
Too much food will make the water dirty.

Watch your goldfish swim to the
top of the water to eat their food.

Cleaning the Tank

It is important to take care of the tank to keep your fish healthy. Every day, check that the water is clean. Every two weeks, clean the entire tank. Ask an adult to help you.

Your goldfish will quickly become sick in a dirty tank.

Use a jug to take out some of the old water.
Put this water into a bucket and place your
goldfish in the bucket. Take out only half of the
old water in the tank. Fill the tank up with
clean water and put the goldfish back in.

Clean any green **algae** off the inside
of the glass with a special sponge.

Growing Up

Goldfish get bigger as they become adults. Watch how big your goldfish grow and make sure that your tank does not get crowded.

Fish that are about three inches (seven centimeters) long are the best size for a tank.

Some types of goldfish can grow to be too big for a small tank. It is best for these goldfish to live in a very large tank or outside in a garden pond. Never let your fish go in a natural pond or lake.

Some parks and zoos have ponds with huge goldfish swimming in them!

A Healthy Goldfish

Goldfish are very healthy pets if you care for them properly. If you think your goldfish looks sick, call a **veterinarian.**

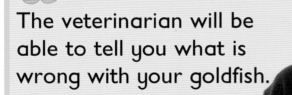

The veterinarian will be able to tell you what is wrong with your goldfish.

If your goldfish is swimming slowly, it may not be healthy. Drooping **fins** or white spots on its skin are also signs of sickness.

If a fish is sick, it is best to move it into a different tank until it is better.

Old Age

If you look after your goldfish well, they can live for many years. They do not need any special care as they get older.

A common goldfish can live for up to 25 years!

Older goldfish should be cared for just like young goldfish. It is still important to keep the tank clean and to feed them every day.

Caring for your fish will help you learn how to treat animals properly.

27

Useful Tips

- Wash your hands before and after you clean the tank or feed your fish.

- Never tap the glass of the tank. This will anger or scare your fish.

- Keep the tank out of reach of cats and other pets.

- Let your goldfish get used to the tank for two weeks before you add more fish.

- When you are cleaning the tank, put your fish in some of the old water in a bucket.

- Never keep your fish in a goldfish bowl. There will not be enough **oxygen** for them to breathe.

Fact File

- Goldfish were first kept as pets by Chinese people over 4,500 years ago.

- The oldest goldfish was thought to be over 50 years old when it died. It lived in China.

- Some common goldfish can grow to be 15 inches (40 centimeters) long.

- Not all goldfish are gold-colored. Some are black, white, or even blue.

- A female goldfish lays 1000 to 3000 eggs at a time.

- Many kinds of goldfish have been raised to have features such as long **fins.**

Glossary

algae tiny plantlike organisms that form a thin, green film on the walls of the tank

filter machine attached to the side of the fish tank to keep the water clean

fins flaps of skin that grow from a fish's sides and back and help it to swim

gills part of a fish's body that takes oxygen from the water so the fish can breathe

gravel tiny rocks

hatch when baby fish come out of their eggs

nutrients things in food that help a fish grow and stay healthy

oxygen gas that animals need to breathe to stay alive

temperature how hot or cold something is

veterinarian doctor who cares for animals

More Books to Read

An older reader can help you with these books.

Barnes, Julia, et al. *101 Facts About Goldfish*. Milwaukee, Wis.: Gareth Stevens, Incorporated, 2002.

Carroll, David. *The ASPCA Complete Guide to Pet Care*. New York: Dutton/Plume, 2001.

Miller, Michaela. *Goldfish*. Chicago: Heinemann Library, 1998.

Walker, Pam. *My Goldfish*. New York: Scholastic Library Publishing, 2001.

Wiebe, Trina, et al. *Goldfish Don't Take Bubble Baths*. Montreal, Quebec: Lobster Press, 2000.

A Note from the ASPCA™

Pets are often our good friends for the very best of reasons. They don't care how we look, how we dress, or who our friends are. They like us because we are nice to them and take care of them. That's what being friends is all about.

This book has given you information to help you know what your pet needs. Learn all you can from this book and others, and from people who know about animals, such as veterinarians and workers at animal shelters like the ASPCA™. You will soon become your pet's most important friend.

Index